Where Were You When She Needed You?

Being A Godly Husband

By Jason Larson

Copyright © 2022 Jason Larson

All rights reserved.

ISBN: 9798847683425
Independently published

DEDICATION

This is dedicated to my beautiful wife, Sarah Larson. She has been such an inspiration to me over the years, especially during the last three years. Even though she is the one going through the physical issues she continues to encourage me. I love you and am proud to still be able to call you, my wife. Sarah not only contributed to this book with support, faith, and encouragement but she also supplied the book cover photo. She took this picture while we were in Alaska the year before her heart attack.

I LOVE YOU SARAH.

SHMILY

CONTENTS

Dedication	ii
Foreword	iv
Acknowledgements	v
Preface	vi
The Godly Husband	1
Faith	22
I Got This	38
You Have Seen My Affliction	48
All Things Work Together for Good	62
To God Be the Glory	86
He's Still Working on Me	100

Foreword

If I had to describe this book in a word, it would be this "a gift." The riches contained within the pages of this real-life account of faith over tragedy, courage over fear, and trust in the one true sovereign God is nothing short of a gift to the body of Christ. I was personally with Jason and Sarah through this and reading the book for the first time not only brought back a rush of emotions for me but also challenged me again to be the husband God has commanded me to be for my wife in holy scripture. I remember telling Jason during the height of this of how he convicted me as a husband and that is still true today. This book will put you on a rollercoaster of emotions as you go page by page into the darkest times of any husband's worst nightmare. Its pages are replete with scripture and offer real hope to the believer. I believe this is exactly what God means for us to do with our tragedies: share them for the glory of God alone and for the edification of the body of Christ.

Soli Deo Gloria

Pastor PJ Pettijohn

ACKNOWLEDGMENTS

Sarah Larson Contributed the cover photo.

Samantha Larson designed the cover

Edited by Dr. Jamie Birdwell

Forword written by Pastor PJ Pettijohn

Preface

Where were you when she needed you:

Physically - Were you home? When you couldn't be, was she on your mind?

Spiritually - Were you the spiritual leader of your home?

Mentally - When you were with her, was she your focus?

I have been asked to share the story of how my wife, Sarah, and I have gone through the most difficult time of our lives and how to love your wife–how to be a Godly husband, and how to keep your faith during these most trying of trials.

My hope is that by the time you finish reading our story, you will have a better understanding of what being a Godly husband means and how making vows to your wife at an altar, before God and men, might someday be put to the ultimate test.

My goal is to brag on God and give you some encouragement, for people to understand that if you have God in your life, you will never go through any hard times alone. On the other hand, if you reject Christ, everything you do, no matter how many people you surround yourself with, will be done alone. Our Savior is our only comfort. When Jesus departed the earth, he sent the Holy Spirit to be our comforter.

I am no great theologian, and I do not have any advanced degrees, but what I do have is our LORD. I have been forged in the fire of life. I have had to learn at breakneck speed to be Godly, have faith, and love my wife the way we are commanded. This takes more than some half-witted commitment. It takes one hundred percent, all in commitment.

I hope when you finish reading this book, you will better understand what it means to be Godly, have strong faith, and love your wife the way we are supposed to. You can learn to trust in God, His sovereignty, and His will; but mostly, I hope we can all learn to give God all the glory all the time.

If I had a theme scripture for this book it would probably be Ephesians 5:25 **Husbands, love your wives, just as Christ loved the church and gave himself up for her.** All scripture is from the English Standard Version unless otherwise indicated.

Chapter 1
The Godly Husband

God has allowed my wife and me to go through a very rough time over the past few years, and, at times, these trials were literally life and death. He has shown Himself to us during this time and has allowed us to learn more about Him and ourselves. Many people have asked me to share what I have learned and what we have gone through. My hope is you will be encouraged by our story.

I have always loved my wife as much as I could. I have loved her to the best of my ability, but probably not as I should have. I have learned a lot about what it means to be a

Godly husband while growing in my faith and learning to control my doubts. You will see I have struggled in these areas immensely during the last three years, and I continue to learn as I study God's word and as He continues to lead and mold me. I have had to surrender everything to God, including the very life of my wife.

The road we have been on has not been easy; we have taken our lumps. I would say we are still taking our lumps, but if God can bring us closer to Him and grow in our love and knowledge of Him, then all is not lost. So, I would like to challenge you as I have been challenged to be a Godlier husband (or man), to grow in your faith, and to control your doubting. The Christian walk was never promised to be easy but is one we walk in faith.

Let me ask, what does it mean to be a Godly husband? This has been a very thought-provoking question and one I have given a lot of attention. I have learned that to be a Godly husband, you must first be Godly, which means we must fully surrender our lives to the Lord. Our very nature is to be ungodly, so we must reject being that, as we see in Titus 2:12

> *For the grace of God has appeared, bringing salvation for all people, training us to renounce ungodliness and worldly passions, and to live self-controlled, upright, and Godly lives in the present age.*

The Cambridge Dictionary[1] defines Godly as obeying and respecting God. We can see that even from a secular point of view, to be Godly, we have to surrender to God.

Next, we need to understand what God desires of us– to accept what He expects of us and be willing to act on it. You must have the indwelling of the Holy Spirit to guide you and direct you (John 16:13). So, if we are striving to be Godly and obeying God, then we need to follow his command to love our wives as Christ loved the church, Ephesians 5:25

---

[1] Godly. (2022). *Cambridge Dictionary*. Retrieved 2022, from https://dictionary.cambridge.org/us/dictionary/english/Godly.

Husbands, love your wives, as Christ loved the church and gave himself up for her.

You must also know God to be a Godly husband, which means we must love because God is love (1 John 4:7-8).

What are some things the world says makes a good husband? These could be things like he makes his wife laugh, makes her feel good about herself, communicates well with her, is faithful to her, compassionate and kind, is mature and works hard. While these are all good qualities in a husband and are qualities we want, being a Godly husband is more than just being a "good" man. Being a Godly husband is a lifetime commitment to God and your wife. Knowing this, we must then know what a Godly husband is not and what he does not do.

Firstly, Godly husbands are not cowards. We look to the earthly father of Jesus, Joseph. Here was a man who was engaged to Mary, whom he later found out was pregnant with a child that was not his. It took great courage - and an angelic visit - for

Joseph to stand by Mary as she was pregnant with Jesus. Being engaged in those days was legally binding, and he and Mary both could have been on the receiving end of harsh punishment from the Jewish leaders of the day. They were, after all, still living under the "Law" and not grace. Joseph was a Godly man, as demonstrated by his willingness to do what God asked of him. He did not lash out. He did not despise Mary, nor is it recorded that he ever spoke ill of her. A man not filled with the Holy Spirit, most certainly, would have responded to such a situation in a much different way.

In Ephesians 5:25, Godly husbands do not rule their families with hatred in their hearts. Let's look at Joseph as an example. Here was a boy so loved by his father that it caused great anger amongst his brothers. So much so that his brothers kidnapped him, threw him into a pit, sold him into slavery, and lied to their father about all of this. Joseph then spent several years in an Egyptian prison because of a lie Pottifer's wife told, about him. I can't imagine it was a great experience. Joseph, in our thinking, probably would have been justified in being angry, maybe even hating his brothers for such cruel acts. Several years later, we see Joseph as the second in command of all Egypt, and his brothers come to him for food during a time of great famine. Joseph did not hate his brothers; instead, he ruled over them with love, giving them the food, they needed despite their previous treatment of him.

    Thirdly, Godly husbands do not attempt to force their wives to be Godly women, but instead lead them spiritually. If we do our job as Godly husbands and abide in Christ, then the rest will fall into place according to God's will and His plan. Proverbs 31:10-31 tells us what a Godly wife is, and as Godly husbands, we should keep this passage in our hearts. Christ has never forced anyone to become part of His bride - the church - and has never forced anyone to be Godly. Instead, He has loved us from the beginning. Romans 5:8 says:

> **But God shows his love for us in that while we were still sinners, Christ died for us.**

Next, Godly husbands do not speak ill of their wives. According to the Apostle Paul, we are to love our wives and not be harsh with them (Colossians 3:19). If we love our wives as we love ourselves, then we would never speak of them or about them in a bad manner. We should hold each other accountable in this area and not allow others to speak poorly about their wives. Instead, we should help our brothers who may be struggling in their marriage and give sound biblical advice.

Now let's look at a few biblical principles that tell us what a Godly husband is and what he is supposed to do according to scripture.

Godly husbands are to be the leaders of their households. We can see this very clearly in Paul's letter to the church at Ephesus.

Ephesians 5:23-24 For the husband is the head of the wife even as Christ is the head of the church, his body, and is himself its Savior. Now as the church submits to Christ, so also wives should submit in everything to their husbands.

We also see a confirmation of this in 1 Corinthians 11:3 **But I want you to understand that the head of every man is Christ, the head of a wife is her husband, and the head of Christ is God.** There are several other scriptures which have similar commands.

How are husbands to lead though? First as servants. We see the example Christ set for us when he was washing the feet of his disciples.

John 13:12-15 When he had washed their feet and put on his outer garments and resumed his place, he said to them, "Do you understand what I have done to you? You call me Teacher and Lord, and you are right, for so I am. If I then, your Lord and Teacher, have washed your feet, you also ought to wash one another's feet. For I have given you an example, that you also should do just as I have done to you."

Secondly, Godly husbands are supposed to lead with love. If we again look at Paul's letter to the Colossians.

Colossians 3:19 Husbands, love your wives, and do not be harsh with them.

Next a Godly husband leads with humility. Paul explains this in his first letter to the Corinthian church.

1 Corinthians 13:4-5 Love is patient and kind; love does not envy or boast; it is not arrogant or rude. It does not insist on its own way; it is not irritable or resentful.

It's important for us to understand this concept because if we do not grasp this principle the rest of what we will talk about will not line up for us. We must also understand that God places such a high expectation on this that our very communication with Him is at stake as Peter tells us in his first letter.

1 Peter 3:7 Likewise, husbands, live with your wives in an understanding way, showing honor to the woman as the weaker vessel, since they are heirs with you of the grace of life, so that your prayers may not be hindered.

Godly husbands follow Christ as the perfect example. Again, the Apostle Paul in Ephesians 5:25-33 tells us explicitly how we should love our wives. In verse 25, Paul tells us that we should love them as Christ loved the church. Jesus is the best example of a Godly husband, the Christ who was all God while being all man (Colossians 2:8-10) loved the Church, His bride, so much He gave his life for her.

Godly husbands also provide for their families. The Bible is very clear on this. There are multiple scriptures that tell us, as husbands and men, that we are to provide for and take care of our families. 1 Timothy 5:8 says that if you do not provide for your family, then you are worse than an unbeliever.

Next, Godly husbands obey God and love their wives unconditionally. In the book of Hosea, we find the story of Hosea the prophet, who was married to a very unfaithful woman who more than likely had children with other men. Hosea continued to love Gomer, was faithful to her, and repeatedly took her back. Although this was an example of the relationship between Israel and God, we can also look to Hosea as a good example of an obedient and Godly husband.

Then, Godly husbands follow God and obey his word. In Genesis 12, we find the story of Abram, who, when God told him to pick up everything and move to a land that

God would show him, Abram did not argue with God. Genesis 12:4 says, "So Abram went..." We, as Godly husbands, must be willing to surrender to the will of God and follow Him where he leads us.

Godly husbands are to seek and completely surrender to God's will continually. Romans 12:2 says,

> **Do not be conformed to this world, but be transformed by the renewal of your mind, that by testing you may discern what is the will of God, what is good and acceptable and perfect.**

This means we are to look to God for our direction. Since we know there are no new revelations, the place we look for God's direction is in His word. The scriptures were given to us so that we may understand what God wants for us and from us. It seems fairly simple when we break it down, but I know, as most everyone else does, this is often easier said than done. I know we must make this an intentional goal each and every day, in every aspect of our lives.

Additionally, Godly husbands sacrifice their time for their families. Again, as we are reminded in Ephesians 5:25, Christ literally laid His life down for us, His bride. He suffered unimaginable pain and heartache on that cruel cross. The Bible tells us in John 10:17b-18

> *I lay down my life that I may take it up again. No one takes it from me, but I lay it down of my own accord. I have authority to lay it down, and I have authority to take it up again. This charge I have received from my Father.*

And since the Apostle Paul commands us to love our wives as Christ loved the church, the only takeaway is that we are to be self-sacrificing. Even if we are never asked to literally lay our lives down for our wives, we must lay aside our own selfish desires. We do not do this for our own vain pride and not so others can pat us on the back. Instead, we, as Godly husbands, want to completely surrender to God's will. We know if God has - through divine intervention and inspiration of the Holy Spirit - allowed for things to be written in the Bible, then it must be part of his will for us.

Being a Godly husband requires love, and 1 Corinthians 13 tells us what love truly is.

> *If I speak in the tongues of men and of angels, but have not love, I am a noisy gong or a clanging cymbal. And if I have prophetic powers, and understand all mysteries and all knowledge, and if I have all faith, so as to remove mountains, but have not love, I am nothing. If I give away all I have, and if I deliver up my body to be burned, but have not love, I gain nothing. Love is patient and kind; love does not envy or boast; it is not arrogant or rude. It does not insist on its own way; it is not irritable or resentful; it does not rejoice at wrongdoing, but rejoices with the truth. Love bears all things, believes all things, hopes all things, endures all things. Love never ends. As for prophecies, they will pass away; as for tongues, they will cease;*

as for knowledge, it will pass away. For we know in part and we prophesy in part, but when the perfect comes, the partial will pass away. When I was a child, I spoke like a child, I thought like a child, I reasoned like a child. When I became a man, I gave up childish ways. For now we see in a mirror dimly, but then face to face. Now I know in part; then I shall know fully, even as I have been fully known. So now faith, hope, and love abide, these three; but the greatest of these is love.

This is such a well-recognized passage and so powerful. It should be our basis for true biblical love and guide for how to love.

There certainly are lots of expectations on what being a Godly husband means. In a world where we have emasculated and perverted what this truly means and have allowed sinfulness and blatant godlessness to prevail, being a Godly husband and man in this world is certainly frowned upon. If you need evidence of this, turn the idiot box (television) on and watch about any program about families and how the father figure is treated and portrayed. He is mostly portrayed as a bumbling idiot and someone who is a laughingstock. If this does not show us how the world is trying to deform what it truly means to be a Godly husband and man, then maybe we should look within and make sure we are not part of this culture.

Now, if you prefer to look at the numbers, then let's look at a 2014 Pew Research Center Study[2]. 66% of the men who participated in this study claimed to be Christians. 57% of the total men surveyed stated they absolutely believe in God, and only 31% said they attend church services of some sort weekly. Some of the most astonishing numbers, to me were that only 30% said there was a clear standard for right and wrong, and 27% said the Bible is the word of God and should be taken literally, but 38% said that the Bible was not the word of God. With beliefs like these, comprising a majority of self-proclaiming Christians, it's no wonder

---

[2] https://www.pewresearch.org/religion/religious-landscape-study/gender-composition/men/

being a Godly husband is seen as being less than manly or otherwise viewed in a negative light.

> *And even if our gospel is veiled, it is veiled to those who are perishing. In their case the god of this world has blinded the minds of the unbelievers, to keep them from seeing the light of the gospel of the glory of Christ, who is the image of God. For what we proclaim is not ourselves, but Jesus Christ as Lord, with ourselves as your servants for Jesus' sake.*
>
> *2 Corinthians 4:3-5*

We have to take a strong stance and not become cowards in the face of all the world has thrown at us. We need to do a Biblical check-up every day and ensure we are still in line with what God would have us, as men and husbands, do. Let's be part of the solution and not part of the problem. If we stay in the Bible and, as the psalmist reminds us in Psalm 119:11: *I have stored up your word in my heart, that I might not sin against you*, then we will be better prepared for what we continue to face on a daily basis.

James 4:14 tells us, "*Yet you do not know what tomorrow will bring. What is your life? For you are a mist that appears for a little time and then vanishes.*" So, with this in mind one of the most important things we can do is to show our sons what a Godly husband is and demonstrate to our daughters what a Godly husband does. We must do all of this so that we might raise future Godly husbands, and wives that will expect their husbands to be Godly. If we fail to prepare our children, then we are setting them up for failure. This is what the devil wants; he wants our children. He wants to destroy us, as we are reminded in 1 Peter 5:8 *Be sober-minded; be watchful. Your adversary the devil prowls around like a roaring lion, seeking someone to devour.*

We need to bear in mind that we must have complete unity with Christ and steer away from the things of this world in order to be Godly husbands. James 4:4

> *You adulterous people! Do you not know that friendship with the world is enmity with God? Therefore whoever wishes to be a friend of the world makes himself an enemy of God.*
> *James 4:4*

Keeping that in mind, we must fight the good fight and run a good race, as the Apostle Paul reminds us in his letters. This is not an easy task, but then again, living the Christian life, in general, is not easy. However, if we commit to being Godly men and Godly husbands, we will truly find great rewards. I think it's safe to say these rewards may not be here on earth but will definitely be heavenly rewards. We are reminded in Matthew 6:19 not to have treasures for ourselves on earth but in Heaven. God never intended for men to be anything less than men. If His intent were different, then His creation would have looked a lot different than it does.

> *God is looking for broken men who have judged themselves in the light of the cross of Christ. When he wants anything done, he takes up men who*

have come to the end of themselves, whose confidence is not in themselves but in God. **Henry Ironside**

When we finally come to our senses and realize that we cannot and will not succeed as Godly men and husbands in and of ourselves, and we must rely on God and God alone to get us through, then and only then will we begin to be prepared for being Godly men and husbands. To get us where we need to be, which is in a place of complete dependence on God, God will sometimes have to bring us to our knees. Then we will be in the correct posture to move forward.

Another unpopular stance is that marriage is forever. Like all married men, I took an oath to my wife before God. This oath went something like this, "I, Jason, take thee, Sarah, to be my wedded wife, to have and to hold from this day forward, for better, for worse, for richer, for poorer, in sickness and in health, to love and to cherish, till death do us part." This, to me, was serious. I would not have made that vow to my wife if I had not actually intended keeping it. What I did not know, and could not have known then, was how much these vows would be tested much later.

I am not the authority on being a Godly husband or being a man of great faith. This is something I constantly work toward and, yes, continually struggle with. However, I have been thrust to my knees through life's circumstances and given a crash course, in real-time, on learning to become a Godlier husband.

The story I have to tell is difficult to repeat and may be difficult to hear, but I think it will help someone, just as going through it has helped me. I continue to learn the basic principle of James 2:12, **Blessed is the man who remains steadfast under trial, for when he has stood the test he will receive the crown of life, which God has promised to those who love him.** I don't know if I will ever have a full grasp of this concept and be able to stay here one hundred percent of the time. I pray for God to help keep my faith strong and keep me looking to him and trusting him for steadfastness, which I believe is just another link in the chain to being a Godly husband.

Chapter 2
FAITH

Faith is necessary to being Godly because a person without faith is not interested in being Godly or in the things of God. So, let's look at what faith is, how we get it, and where it comes from.

What is faith? The best place to find this answer is in the word of God. In Hebrews chapter 11, verse 1, Paul tells what faith is, ***"Now faith is the assurance of things hoped for, the conviction of things not seen."*** Here "conviction" can be replaced with the word evidence; the King James version uses the word "evidence." According to the freedictionary.com[3], evidence is *ground for belief or disbelief; data on which to base proof or to establish truth or falsehood.* In this case, faith is evidence for things we cannot see with our physical body.

Now, what does it take to have faith? Romans 4:11-12 says

This Jesus is the stone that was rejected by you, the builders, which has become the cornerstone. And there is salvation in no one else, for there is no other name under heaven given among men by which we must be saved.

For us to have saving faith, we must believe in the substitutionary sacrifice of Christ to atone for our sins. Once this is established, the rest will fall into place, such as our faith in God's promises, faith in God's sovereignty, and faith in God as the one true God. This belief is central to Christianity, and without a firm belief in this principle, a person cannot go any further into the idea of having saving faith because he has disbelief in his heart. When

---

[3] https://www.thefreedictionary.com/evidence

Christ died on the cross for our sins, He paid the price for all past, present, and future sins, even doubt. This, however, is not a license to sin. As Paul reminds us in his letter to the Romans in chapter 6, verses one and two, we do not need to sin more so that grace can abound more.

The next question is, where does faith come from? Romans 12:3 tells us:

For by the grace given to me I say to everyone among you not to think of himself more highly than he ought to think, but to think with sober judgment, each according to the measure of faith that God has assigned.

This verse leaves no room for any questions about the origin of our faith or who is the author of our faith. Then we find in Ephesians 2:8-9 that faith leads to salvation,

For by grace you have been saved through faith. And this is not your own doing; it is the gift of God, not a result of works, so that no one may boast.

Since faith comes from God and salvation is His gift to us, that means we did absolutely nothing to earn faith or salvation. That must then mean there is nothing we can do to lose our faith or salvation, not even having doubt. This is a struggle I found myself in at times during the last three years. I had lots of doubt and wavering faith. I never doubted who God was or what He did for us. I guess it was doubt that God could, or would, actually bring us through everything we had went through and are continuing to go through, which is a promise from God that we find throughout scripture.

During these times, I reminded myself that doubt was not blasphemy, and it was not a cause for losing something that wasn't mine to lose—my faith. I knew I had belief, a strong belief in God and what He has done for us. Sometimes we find ourselves in dark places and seem to like it for one reason or another and tend to camp out there living in ourself-pity. I certainly found myself there more often than I would like to admit. I'm reminded of

James 1:5-8, which says

> *If any of you lacks wisdom, let him ask God, who gives generously to all without reproach, and it will be given him. But let him ask in faith, with no doubting, for the one who doubts is like a wave of the sea that is driven and tossed by the wind. For that person must not suppose that he will receive anything from the Lord; he is a double-minded man, unstable in all his ways.*

What does this mean whenever we have doubt? To be double-minded sounds like that person would have two masters. We cannot trust God and not trust Him at the same time. This makes us double-minded.

With this in mind, I think we can better understand that doubt does not cause us to lose salvation or faith; however, it is sin and something over which we need to gain control and ask forgiveness. Romans 14:23 tells us *But whoever has doubts is condemned if he eats, because the eating is not from faith. For whatever does not proceed from*

faith is sin. I found myself continually asking for forgiveness for my doubt. Still, I was comforted by the fact God will continue to forgive us as 1 John 1:9 tells us: ***If we confess our sins, he is faithful and just to forgive us our sins and to cleanse us from all unrighteousness.***

It may seem like I am the bearer of bad news, talking about doubt, but it gives me great comfort and hope to know that in my most feeble moments of doubt and discouragement God is there for me and the Holy Spirit comforts me. We have assurance during these times found in Psalm 94:18-19. ***If I should say, "My foot has slipped," Your lovingkindness, O Lord, will hold me up. When my anxious thoughts multiply within me, Your consolations delight my soul*** (NASB).

There are differences between doubt and disbelief. Only a believer can have doubt about things biblical because a person cannot doubt something he doesn't already believe. Then, only an unbeliever can have disbelief because a believer, by its very definition, believes. The Cambridge Dictionary defines doubt as *"a feeling of not being certain about something, especially about how good or true it is*[4]*"*. Cambridge defines disbelief as *"the feeling of not being able to believe that something is true or real.*[5]*"*

Having identified the difference between doubt and disbelief, there is also a precise difference between doubting your salvation versus doubting what you believe to be true about a particular circumstance. We can look at Peter in Matthew 14. This is where Jesus allowed Peter to walk on the water, but when Peter noticed the storm and the waves around him, he took his eyes off of the Lord and began sinking. This could be us during any time of difficulty in our lives. Here Peter cried out to Jesus for help. Just as Jesus immediately reached out his hand to lift Peter up out of the troubled seas, He will help us today when we cry out to Him. Jesus

---

[4] Doubt. (2022). *Cambridge Dictionary*. Retrieved 2022, from
https://dictionary.cambridge.org/us/dictionary/english/doubt.

[5] Disbelief. (2022). *Cambridge Dictionary*. Retrieved 2022, from
https://dictionary.cambridge.org/us/dictionary/english/doubt.

attributed Peter's sinking in the water to doubt and having little faith. I think we can all agree that Peter's belief and loyalty to Christ were not lost because of his doubt.

We have now established the fact that there is a definitive difference between disbelief and doubt. Disbelief will most certainly send our souls to hell, but doubt will not. Doubt comes into play when God's will and timing do not align themselves with our will or timing. It seems to me that doubt generally occurs when Christians lose hope during a certain time in our lives but do not lose our faith in Christ. Disbelief is a condition of the heart. More plainly put, disbelief is the rejection of Christ.

Now let's look at a couple of stark contrasts between two men in the Bible, one had disbelief, and the other had doubt. Judas, who betrayed our LORD for thirty pieces of silver, is a great example of not having belief in God. In Acts 1:25, we see where Peter said, of Judas, that he went to his *"own place."* In John 6:70-71, Jesus, speaking of Judas, called him a devil. The original Greek word used for devil here is diabolos, which is the same word used in Matthew 4:8, where the devil is tempting Jesus in the wilderness. Based on these scriptures, it is safe to say Judas's "*own place*" is hell, as hell is meant for Satan, his demons, and unbelievers. We find this in II Peter 2:4-9.

On the other side of the disbelief verses doubt coin, we look at Thomas (also known as "Doubting Thomas"). Here we see someone who walked with Christ and saw the many miracles Jesus performed, yet he doubted but was not cast aside by our Lord. Jesus did, however, give us great hope. In John 20:29, Jesus, speaking to Thomas, **said to him, "Have you believed because you have seen me? Blessed are those who have not seen and yet have believed."**

We have some great examples of how doubting a particular situation is not the same as disbelief or even doubting your salvation. I think it's important to look at some examples of people who had great faith but sometimes had a certain amount of doubt.

Let's look at Abraham. In Genesis

Chapter 22, we find the story of Abraham taking Isaac, his son, up the mountain to be a sacrifice. Verse 1 of this chapter says that God tested Abraham. I've heard it said, "A faith that cannot be tested is one that cannot be trusted." Peter talks about testing the genuineness of our faith, and that the testing is more precious than gold (1 Peter 1:6-7). Abraham's faith was strong enough that when Isaac asked about the sacrifice needed, Abraham responded by telling him that God would provide the sacrifice. Because of his faith, God stopped Abraham and provided a sacrifice by way of a ram in the thicket.

When we read this passage, we do not see anywhere that Abraham had any doubt. However, if we look earlier in Abraham's life, there were two different times he told men in powerful positions that Sarah, his wife, was his sister. Then we see how much doubt both Abraham and Sarah had when God told them He was going to give them a son. In Genesis 16, we see the story of Hagar and Ishmael. During these times, I think it's safe to say Abraham suffered from uncertainty and doubt. When we look at Abraham's faith and doubt, it comforts us that even one of the greatest men of the Bible had the same issue with doubt that we have. So, when we go through trials or seem to be camped out in the valley and are only able to look up to the mountain tops, we can remember that we were not alone in the area of doubt. God has not given up on us because we have doubt.

Then when we look at Moses, we see his faith dotted all over the first five books of the Bible. From choosing to be an Israelite rather than being called a son of Pharaoh or confronting Pharaoh and demanding that God's people be set free, or leaving Egypt for the vast wilderness, or when he lifted his hand and staff over the Red Sea, and it parted. I don't think anyone will argue that Moses had faith, even during some very hard times. However, prior to all of this, Moses had doubts. The two most prominent examples are after he killed the Egyptian soldier when he fled into a foreign country.; Later, we see it when God approached him in the burning bush, he begged God to pick someone else because he doubted. Moses's doubt did not cause him to lose his place in heaven among the saints.

If God didn't expect us to have doubt, he would not have provided so many scriptures about living with and overcoming doubt. God is faithful to us and continually works in our lives if we do our part to live for Him. The greatest comfort is found in Isaiah 41:10. **Fear not, for I am with you; be not dismayed, for I am your God; I will strengthen you, I will help you, I will uphold you with my righteous hand.**

The events of the last several years have tested my faith, and I have dealt with many doubts. I had to continually study and remind myself that doubt was normal and that in doubting, I was not losing my faith in Christ. I only needed to repent. You see, my wife, Sarah, and I have been dealing with such hard times that any attempt to describe them would almost be futile. So, hoping I can help someone who is, has, or will go through unbearably hard times, I will try to impress on you how great and awesome God truly is, how faithful He is and how loving He is even when we don't deserve it.

In the coming chapters, I will tell how my wife Sarah and I have endured the trial of a lifetime with God's help. This story is truly a love story, one of how God truly loves us, brings us through the hard times, and keeps us safe in His loving arms. A story of how you actually can grow to love your wife more, even after 25 years of marriage. I will hopefully demonstrate how we can become better husbands, Godlier in our role as husbands, even though we have doubt at times, all the while having life thrown in our face.

Through our story you will also see just how great God's timing is. It may rarely be on our time, but God's timing is perfect even if we must continually keep our doubts in check. I will also try to show how God's grace and mercy give us strength as needed. We have all heard that God will not give us more than we can handle. The truth lies in the following scriptures:

> *No temptation has overtaken you that is not common to man. God is faithful, and He will not let you be tempted beyond your ability, but with the temptation He will also provide the way of escape, that you may be able to endure it. 1 Corinthians 10:13*

> *I can do all things through Him who strengthens me. Philippians 4:13*

This tells us that, while He will not give us more than we can handle, it is not talking about doing anything by ourselves. A lot of people forget that there is more to the verse.

Our story will also show that God has not left us, and He is still with us. Joshua 1:9 says,

> *Have I not commanded you? Be strong and courageous. Do not be frightened, and do not be dismayed, for the Lord your God is with you wherever you go.*

I don't think our story is too different from most others, but maybe some can gain inspiration or encouragement from what we have gone through. I will try to express how God has allowed us to maintain our faith through this and how God has brought us through such hard times. How God enables us to look at this time as a blessing more than anything else, and without God, this is an impossible place to be, let alone an impossible place to stay.

I strongly feel that if we do not share our struggles and how God has brought us through them, we are missing the bigger picture and purpose for being allowed to be carried through them. I believe God has brought us through this time in our lives so that we would be able to share with others just how great God truly is, how faithful God is, and how much he loves us.

I want to emphasize that this in no way is meant to brag on my family or me. This is only intended to brag about God. I have been asked to share this so other may know about our story, and so I ask you to learn with me what it means to be a Godlier husband.

Chapter 3
I Got This

    I grew up in the panhandle of Florida, while Sarah grew up in the pacific northwest in Tacoma, Washington. After high school and taking some time trying to figure out what I wanted to be when I grew up, I joined the United States Army in November of 1992 and attended basic training at Fort McClellan, Alabama. Just before graduation, we received orders for our permanent duty stations. My orders were sending me to jump school at Fort Benning, Georgia. Later, these orders were changed, and I was headed to Fort Lewis, Washington (just outside of Tacoma, Washington). Now understand, until now, I had never been west of the Mississippi River, so this was sure to be an adventure.

In March of 1993, I reported to Fort Lewis, Washington. This was great. The weather was unusual for me, and the people were different (not in a bad way, just a different way). Even the smells were different. It took some time to adjust, but not too long, because I quickly learned there were several lakes near my barracks. Because I am someone who loves fishing, this was great news. I also learned making friends in the Army was very easy. Everyone was always moving around, so it was natural to meet new people all the time.

In May of 1993, Sarah and I met for the first time. It didn't take us long to realize we were meant for each other. Less than a month later, the Army sent me to Ft. Wainwright, Alaska, for most of June. This would be the first of many months spent away from the love of my life.

We married in February of 1994; we later learned there was a bet among the family on how long we would be married. The longest was not much more than a year or so, as I have been told. We sure showed them. As of February 2022, we have been married for 28 glorious years and going for as long as she will allow me. Just a few days after we married, my Army unit was set to deploy to the country of Panama, so Sarah and I stayed in a local hotel for the weekend as our honeymoon. Sarah routinely says of the Panama deployment that I went on our honeymoon without her. I would spend the next four months in Panama, and this was hard. Our daughter was born while I was there, so I could not be present for her birth. This was just another example of Sarah's toughness and fierce independence.

Sarah has a lot of great qualities. Sarah is strong mentally and physically. Being a soldier's wife was not an easy task for anyone. Very often, she was more like a single mother, since the Army would constantly send us on training exercises and deployments. These would be anywhere from a weekend "camping trip" to half a year-long deployment.

Once out of the Army, we moved back to the panhandle of Florida, where I joined my local sheriff's office, during which I would have, in my opinion, an awesome career. Again, being the wife of a law enforcement officer was no easy tasking. There was the shift work, the endless days of coming home late because of the late calls. There was constantly being on call for this event or that disaster, and there was working all the overtime so we could live on a lawman's salary. Later, there were the transfers to investigations and promotions that would give me less and less time at home, but in true fashion, Sarah would handle all of this like the hero she was and is.

Through all this, Sarah did a great job raising our two children and keeping our home somewhat sane. She rarely took jobs that were not at the school where the kids were attending. She never wanted the kids to be "latch-key kids." She was home with them in the evenings, taking care of them and our home while I seemed to always be working. I hear all the time how law enforcement folks are heroes, but in my most humble opinion, my wife was the biggest hero of all. I would always remind her of this, which she hated.

One of Sarah's qualities that stuck out the most early on in our lives was her independence. Sarah was, in fact, the most independent person I had ever met. She never feared "going at it alone" or taking on a new challenge and personified the very essence of independence.

I remember once we were in the process of putting a fence around our first home. I was working shift work at the time and had not gotten many of the wooden fence posts in before having to go to work for the evening. I later received a call from our neighbor telling me Sarah was digging fence post holes with a shovel. I asked her why she was using a shovel instead of the post-hole diggers, and she said she knew how the shovel worked, not the post-hole diggers. This was Sarah, she's very determined, and if you told her she couldn't do something, she was going to show you eight different ways she could. This was just one example of how independent and determined Sarah is. What I did not know was just how much of a benefit this trait would be later on.

I had dedicated my life to public service, first in the Army, then at the sheriff's office where I retired in November of 2017, while Sarah had dedicated her life to our family. She is selfless, hard-working, loving and a great homemaker.

Sarah dreamed of going to Alaska for much of our life together. She loves the idea of being in the wide-open country and being around all the animals; mostly, she loves the idea of the weather. She loves seeing landscapes on television. She enjoys the colder weather and the idea of being able to smell, what I told her was, the freshness of the air up there. She loved the thought of going to Alaska so much that I promised to take her when I retired. So, upon me retiring, we went on a cruise to Alaska. She was as happy as I remember ever seeing her. She absolutely loved all things. This trip did not disappoint, so much so that she threatened to stay at every port we went to. There were many times I thought I might have to actually drag her back onto the ship.

    This would have been the summer of 2018 and very near our 25th wedding anniversary. It was the most memorable vacation of all time. Sarah actually referred to this as our honeymoon, as we never had an actual honeymoon. Remember the weekend in the hotel?

    In August of 2019, we visited her family in Washington state. We stayed at the best little bed and breakfast near the water. We had a great time visiting her family and seeing all the sights that a tourist would see. Mostly, we enjoyed just being in each other's company and not having to worry about any schedule. This would later become a very important trip for us, at least for me it would be. I even planned an elk hunt in Colorado for October 2019. I was supposed to leave on October 9, 2019, a very important date. This was a "bucket list" hunt for me. I was so looking forward to this hunt that I could not think of much more for several months.

    Sarah and I were enjoying my retirement. I was making lots of money in my real estate business, and it seemed like a great retirement job for someone who was not ready to be fully retired. I accomplished a lot, and I bought what I wanted to buy when I wanted to buy it. I was on top of the world, doing what I wanted. I... I... I... Notice the theme here was not God but a very self-centered I. I definitely had cut God out of my life and depended solely on me. I put God on a shelf in my mind and did not keep Him in the prominent position He needed to be, I had a very low opinion of God and a very high opinion of myself. This type of backwards thinking will always lead us to be in the wrong place in our Christian walk, which, I can say with the utmost confidence, is where I found myself in 2019.

    I was in a place where I needed a reality check. Little did I know what the very near future held for Sarah and me. I do not want to say that we were going to be punished for any wrongdoing, but in John 15:1-2 Jesus tells us:

I am the true vine, and my Father is the vinedresser. Every branch in me that does not bear fruit he takes away, and every branch that does bear fruit he prunes, that it may bear more fruit.

Safe to say, I was not bearing much fruit for the Gospel.

It's funny how we can look back on a situation and see things more clearly. I can look back to 2018 and 2019 and see how things were not lined up as they should have been. Oh sure, I was not living a life full of sinful desires and acts. It's not a sin to go on vacation with your wife or to go on the dream hunt of a lifetime, and it's not a sin to earn a decent living or to enjoy life. We are never commanded to live dull, boring lives and never have fun. But when you do not have God as the center of your life, and you are not living your life for Him, but for yourself, then that is a sin.

1 John 2:15-17 Do not love the world or the things in the world. If anyone loves the world, the love of the Father is not in him. For all that is in the world—the desires of the flesh and the desires of the eyes and pride of life—is not from the Father but is from the world. And the world is passing away along with its desires, but whoever does the will of God abides forever.

Today I have to be in constant prayer that I may keep my eyes on Christ and keep Christ the center of my life. We can all agree, I'm sure, that we do not want to disobey God, but when we do what we want and leave God out of it, that is complete disobedience to God and His commands for our lives. The one prayer that I have to pray every day is for God to make me a better husband; not the husband I think I should be or even the husband maybe my wife thinks I should be, but the husband God wants me to be. This has to be a daily surrender to God's will for me; somehow, I do not think I am alone in this.

Chapter 4
You Have Seen My Affliction

Sometime in the early fall of 2019, Sarah had developed what was believed to be bronchitis. This was not uncommon for her, and she would get this at least once or twice a year, generally in the spring and fall. She did her usual, and she called "Teladoc" which was provided by her new employer (she had just left an employer who provided health insurance for a less stressful job that did not provide health insurance). The doctor prescribed a round of antibiotics, which did not seem to help much. She later scheduled an appointment with our family physician, who again prescribed her antibiotics. This usually knocked bronchitis out in just a matter of days. This time, though, it seemed to linger.

During the evening October 5, 2019, Sarah came to me and said, "I'm not doing well; I need to go to the hospital." I noticed she was having a hard time breathing. For Sarah to ask to go to the hospital was highly unusual. She handled everything with her typical strength, so when she asked, I knew immediately this was serious. We instantly got into the truck and began heading to our local hospital. We did not make it past the first fire station. As a retired deputy sheriff, I knew many of the local firemen, and I also knew most of them were highly trained emergency medical technicians or paramedics. I pulled into the fire station in hopes they were not currently on a call. They had actually just returned back to the fire station from a call. Did you see God's timing there? One of the firemen was a very good friend of mine. He immediately began treating Sarah after I told him what was going on. He stated that an ambulance would be the best way to get

Sarah to the hospital, so an ambulance was called and transported Sarah to the hospital.

While at the hospital, the medical staff, who were very caring, ran many tests on Sarah. They took x-rays and did breathing treatments. Ultimately, she was treated for bronchitis and released early the next morning. Sarah began feeling better and could go to work the following Monday. She was only able to work for half a day, then she became very fatigued and needed to come home. At the time, I was working as a real estate agent and had a very flexible schedule, allowing me to be able to come home early and help Sarah.

When I came home, my sweet, sweet Sarah was actually making some diabetic-friendly cookies for me to take with me on my Colorado elk hunt. I had been diagnosed with diabetes the previous year and had to make a drastic lifestyle change, so Sarah found a cookie recipe for me. You see, when Sarah was growing up, her grandfather hunted for elk in the mountains of Washington state every October, and her grandmother would make him "hunting cookies." Sarah wanted to do this for me. "Ain't" she awesome, y'all!!!

Later that night we did our nightly routine and got ready for bed. Sarah planned on working the next day, Tuesday, October 8, 2019. This is the morning our world changed forever, and my faith was shaken. Sarah woke me up around 5:15 a.m. by screaming my name. You know when you hear a loved one's voice, and you can immediately tell something is not right. Well, that is exactly what I heard in Sarah's voice. I knew instantly she was not okay. I jumped out of bed and ran into the bathroom where she was. She asked me if she looked okay. *It's 5:15 in the morning, and you just yelled my name to ask me if you look, okay?* This is my passing thought, but I still knew something was wrong. She told me she felt fuzzy and couldn't breathe.

From my years in law enforcement, I have been to these types of calls. I knew without any doubt Sarah was in medical distress. I called 911, which was a foreign thing for me because for so many years, I was 911. In my demanding and commanding sergeant's voice, I began explaining to the very nice and professional dispatcher what I needed and how I needed it to happen. This is what I was used to doing in an emergency situation.

I told the dispatcher I needed an ambulance and explained my wife was having great difficulty breathing. I also explained that her condition was fading quickly, and I needed the ambulance 10-18, which is a police officer talk in our area for I need the ambulance here yesterday. I also explained I needed the closest deputy to respond. She politely asked why I would need a deputy for a medical call. I told her that I felt a deputy might be closer and could certainly drive faster; I did not intend to do CPR on my wife by myself. It would not hit me until sometime later, maybe my drive to the hospital or maybe at the hospital, that this was happening to us. This was not a call I was on; this was happening to my wife. This was the kind of thing that happens to other people, not to us.

Once I was confident the ambulance and deputy were on the way, I hung up from that call, and began calling our adult children (who lived just around the block). I also called one of my dear neighbor friends, who I was confident would handle himself appropriately in an emergency.

My neighbor friend arrived first and was standing by for me to bark orders for what we were going to do. My daughter arrived shortly thereafter and was getting the dogs outside and preparing an unobstructed way for the paramedics to get into my bedroom.

Once the paramedics arrived, they brought in the stretcher and other necessary equipment. I briefly explained to them what was going on. They must have noticed how dire things were because one of the paramedics immediately began attending to Sarah and asked her what her name was. Sarah answered this question, and then she collapsed. This is when my wife died—right there in our bedroom. The paramedics put her on the stretcher and told me they were going to have to intubate Sarah. I, still in lawman mode, said something to the extent of "Son if you're waiting for my approval, you're wasting time, do whatever you have to do to save my wife".

They were very gracious and did all they could for Sarah; they intubated her and ran to the ambulance with her on a stretcher. They worked on her for the next six minutes, all of which she was dead. She had no pulse, was not breathing, and had no signs of life. After six minutes, with the help of God, they were able to revive Sarah. I strongly believe that God had kept Sarah conscious until the paramedics arrived, so they were witnesses to her "fall" (the term used when a person loses consciousness or dies). I also believe this is why they worked so very hard to revive her.

When the paramedics left for the hospital with Sarah, they lost her several more times, and God's perfect grace brought her back every time. I waited for a few minutes before leaving the house to go to the hospital. I knew the ambulance needed to get there without me hindering them. I also know myself and knew I would not be able to drive safely had I followed them.

My daughter and I began driving to the hospital within just a few minutes. The drive was packed with phone calls to all the family members, local and distant; and somehow, I even decided to call the dispatcher I had initially called and apologized to her for being demanding. She was very gracious and told me I had no reason to apologize. I called our pastor, who was out of town at a conference. He arranged for one of the church elders to meet me at the hospital.

I really do not even remember the drive to the hospital. However, once at the emergency room, my daughter and I went to the front desk clerk, and I demanded they let us in to see my wife. The poor lady, who only showed up that day to do her job and gather a paycheck, did not know what kind of sheepdog she was really talking to when she told me "No." I am not certain what my response was, but I do know the next person I was speaking to was the security guard. He was a kind gentleman and made arrangements for me to get my daughter and me to where Sarah was, which was a trauma room. I was not necessarily proud of how I talked with certain people that day, but my hope and prayer is they knew I meant no ill will toward them.

Maybe you can or cannot imagine what I saw when I got to the trauma room. More medical professionals were working on Sarah than I could count or even wanted to count. They had her hooked up to an assortment of monitors and other equipment required to keep her alive. They had her intubated, and that tube was coming out of her mouth. There were Iv's, heart monitors, and an array of other monitors hooked up. I was immediately taken off to the side, where the doctors had a lot of questions regarding her medical history and what exactly happened leading up to this.

I answered everything the best I could and had to keep taking breaks to peer in on Sarah. I only wanted this nightmare to end and for us to wake up and everything be okay. I was constantly praying. Obviously, I was praying for Sarah, I was also praying for strength, and I was praying for my kids. By this time, my son and his wife had arrived at the hospital, along with the elder from the church, one of the sweetest and strongest men I know and a retired law enforcement officer.

I do not remember all the people I spoke with, but several friends, co-workers and past co-workers showed up at the emergency room within what seemed like minutes of me getting there. I know we had a lot of people praying for us, and I felt the immediate comfort of our Savior. I am reminded of what the psalmist said in Psalm 31:7-8,

> *I will rejoice and be glad in your steadfast love, because you have seen my affliction; you have known the distress of my soul, and you have not delivered me into the hand of the enemy; you have set my feet in a broad place.*

Thank God, He does not leave us to suffer alone. If anyone knows anything about suffering, it would be our Lord, and He is there with us during our trials and tribulations.

The rest of the day was mostly a whirlwind of activity and questions. The doctors approached me about putting Sarah on a cold ice machine (layman's terms). The idea was to intentionally put Sarah into a state of hypothermia to protect her vital organs from any damage resulting from her medical condition. The cardiologist told me Sarah's heart was not operating at 100%, and the other attending physicians warned me about getting my hopes up for Sarah's survival.

At this point, I knew a few things. 1. Sarah's ejection fraction (the amount of blood pumped with each beat of the heart) was at 10%. The doctors told me this was not something she could heal from and not something she would live from without some sort of medical intervention. 2. I knew Sarah had died for at least six minutes, and God brought her back. This resulted in an anoxic brain injury, a direct result of the lack of oxygen to her brain. 3. She was in a coma. She had slipped into a natural coma, and we did not know when, or if, she would wake up from it. 4. We were looking at a long stay in the hospital. The medical staff had no idea what exactly happened but knew it was not good. The doctors told me her ability to survive this was bleak, and again, I should not get my hopes up. 5. Most importantly, we serve an awesome and mighty God, who is not confined to our limited knowledge and ability.

The doctors, by now, determined that Sarah had gone into respiratory distress, which caused her to go into cardiac arrest. They kept telling me not to get my hopes up and that her condition was critical and serious. They told me initially she might not make it through the night.

Do you remember Joshua 1:9, where God promised to never leave us nor forsake us? All I could do was pray. Pray for strength, pray for Sarah's recovery, pray for God to somehow comfort me and tell me everything was going to be okay. I felt a strange sense of comfort, almost like a constant hug. I felt like God was right there with me, with His hand on my shoulder encouraging me. I knew this was not literal, but it was certainly comforting. I hesitate to say prayer was all I had, but it is what we have been given by grace— a direct line of communication to our Lord and Savior. He did not forget who we were. To the contrary, out of the billions and billions of people on the planet, God looked down and saw two poor souls and felt enough compassion to heal our hearts and comfort us.

> *Rejoice in the Lord always; again I will say, rejoice. Let your reasonableness be known to everyone. The Lord is at hand; do not be anxious about anything, but in everything by prayer and supplication with thanksgiving let your requests be made known to God. And the peace of God, which surpasses all understanding, will guard your hearts and your minds in Christ Jesus. Philippians 4:4-7*

I would love to tell you that I had such steadfast faith that I did not waiver in my belief in God's ability to carry us through this and in God's ability to heal Sarah. The truth was that my faith was on the same rollercoaster ride that I was on. It was up and down. I needed to get grounded somehow, and I could not figure this out or make sense of it. I still do not know if I can make complete sense of all of this, but God does love us, and he does take care of us in our hour of need.

Humble yourselves, therefore, under the mighty hand of God so that at the proper time he may exalt you, casting all your anxieties on him, because he cares for you. 1 Peter 5:6-7

I will tell you this was so much easier said than done, but once I was able to get my mind around the fact that God does care (there are so many other scriptures that tell us He does), I was able to calm myself down.

Chapter 5
All Things Work Together for Good

By the end of day 1, October 8, Sarah had been moved to the ICU (Intensive Care Unit). She was hooked up to machines to help her breathe, heart monitors, blood pressure monitors, oxygen sensors, and this "cold ice" machine. She did not have anything hooked up to help her heartbeat, and her brain activity was unknown at the time.

Like most married couples, we talked about each other's wishes should we be in a position where we would have to be on life support. I knew Sarah did not want to live on life support, and she did not want to live on life support machines all day, every day. At this point, I did not have enough information to determine if this was the case and thus far, the doctors wanted to give Sarah every chance to live. Little did I know how short-lived that attitude would be.

Sarah would ultimately be in a coma for ten days. This was the absolute toughest time in my life. I had to make sure that I held myself together for our children, although they seemed to give me strength most of the time. I had to make sure I was lucid enough to answer questions from the hospital staff. Sarah would have around six doctors. There was the Hospitalist, the Cardiologist, the Pulmonologist, the Internist, the Neurologist, and the infectious disease doctor. All of them had their questions, and all of them had their priority. I felt like all their priorities were valid and needed attention. So, I wanted to be sure I could answer all their questions.

I did not leave the hospital for the first couple of weeks. Don't worry, the staff was great and allowed me to shower in the doctor's locker room. After the first couple of weeks, I would only leave to go to church. I needed the comfort of our church family, to be in God's house, and to know that God was still there. Sometimes I felt like He was not. This was when I realized I had stepped away from God, and He had not left me at all. I would have to quickly correct myself on this and make sure I kept my eyes on the cross. This is the only time I felt any peace. Other than that, I would have anxiety issues and would not be able to have any clear thoughts. I knew family was there for me also. My parents and Sarah's mother were great and very punctual about visiting. It was just a matter of getting my mind and heart right.

    During these ten days, I continually heard a small voice saying, "My will." This was all day, every day, to the point that I thought I was going crazy. Our Pastor had come up to the hospital, if not twice a day, at least once a day. I shared this only with him, I needed someone to tell me I was not crazy. Of course, he plainly told me that was not the reason I was crazy. I knew exactly who was asking this of me. Yet somehow, I could not agree to let go of any control I thought I might have. I knew this might mean that I could actually lose Sarah. I guess I had it in my head that if I did not consent to the will of God, then I would not lose Sarah, I am not sure where this came from, but it was my thought. This was the first time I really had any thought of the fact that I might actually lose Sarah. After all that has been happening, this is what it would take for me to realize that I actually could lose my wife. I could not agree to this. I would argue about this in my head as though I had any control over it.

I am ultra-aware of the "Lord's Prayer" found in Matthew 6 and Luke 11, here Jesus says, "...Thy will be done on earth as it is in heaven." I could not bring myself to this point. I knew I had no control over whether Sarah lived or not, but in my finite mind, if I did not agree with God's will, then I would not face the prospect of losing her. Weird thoughts, I know, but as people, we do not always have the most understandable ideas in times of crisis. Martin Luther is quoted as saying, "A Christian is never in a state of completion but always in a process of becoming." I like to think that I was in a state of becoming more and more reliant on God and looking for His comfort in my life, especially at this dire time.

Not many days passed before the doctors began telling me how hopeless Sarah's condition was. They began hinting that, in their opinion, the right thing to do would be to take Sarah off all supportive measures. They would later be more direct and constant in voicing their "medical opinion." Again, I would love to tell you that I had rock-solid faith, but I would be lying to you. There were times when I would feel like I was on an island all by myself, and the island was sinking. I would wonder where God was, where my family was, and where my friends were. Most nights, if I could sleep, I would cry myself to sleep. I would have to constantly remind myself, with the help of Godly people, that God had not left me, but I kept creeping away from God.

I had been sleeping in those very "comfortable" hospital recliners (note the sarcasm). Sometimes, I would pull the recliner next to Sarah's bed. A few nights, I would see shadows moving around, not too uncommon as people were moving around all the time. Then one night, I really could not sleep because of the shadows moving near the front of the hospital room, I got up and sat on the couch by the side wall of the room directly across from the bathroom. I looked up at Sarah's bed and noticed angels surrounding her bed. They were not what I would call peacemakers. These angels were dressed for battle. It appeared to be as though they were actually protecting Sarah from any harm, whether it be physical or spiritual harm. This actually gave me great comfort and peace. Sarah would later tell me she, too, saw the angels surrounding her bed. She would say that it seemed impossible for such large beings to fit into a hospital room. This is very significant for Sarah to say as you will see later on.

On about day ten, that small voice inside my head was getting more and more persistent, "My will. My will". I could hardly bear it anymore. My pastor was in the room later on this day. He and I were talking when I heard Sarah say my name. This was a literal impossibility as she still had the intubation tube in her throat. I looked at the pastor and asked if he had heard this. He looked at me weirdly, which I was used to at this point, and said he did not hear anything. I told him that Sarah just called my name. I got up from my seat, walked over to her bed and looked at her. I began crying as I noticed she did not say anything; she was still in a coma. The persistent "My Will" inside my head and the thoughts of never seeing my wife alive again, I finally prayed, "Okay, God, Your Will, but if You are going to take her, please don't let her suffer. Take her quickly. But if you are going to leave her here, then please restore her completely." I heard a voice as plain as any voice I have ever heard say "She will be okay; there will be something left." I looked at the pastor and said please tell me you heard that. He again looked at me like I had half a dozen eyes on my forehead and said he did not hear anything. I could only sit down and cry. I did not and do not want to hear that voice again. It scared me yet comforted me. I could not engage the voice, as I knew it was the voice of God.

I felt this was the absolute worst place to be, thinking I had just signed Sarah's death certificate. Immediately I knew differently because Sarah came out of her coma. The nurses came in and began calling doctors. After making sure Sarah was responsive, they put her back on a sedative to keep her from taking the intubation tube out of her mouth. The doctors continued to caution me that Sarah was not out of the woods yet, and the possibility of her surviving was very slim. I was presented with a "DNR", a Do Not Resuscitate Order. I was told that if something else happened to Sarah, things would be much more severe. I agreed with this and did not want Sarah to endure anything further, so I signed the "DNR." You talk about difficulty. This was hard. Here I am telling the doctors, telling the world that if something else happens to my beloved, I do not want any life-saving measures to be taken. I truly felt this was the best thing in light of all that had occurred.

I tried my best to keep a diary of everything happening and my thoughts as things were happening. I was writing this in the event Sarah did not make it so I could remember how things happened. I kept a diary so that I could remember the raw emotion of my feelings and thoughts while we were in the hospital. I stopped keeping the diary after I heard God's voice. Some of this may seem like rambling and some of it may not exactly line up with what I have already written, as it was all a blur at the time. When you are in the midst of a crisis, you do not necessarily remember exactly how things happen but later have better clarity. Obviously, these things were not written as they happened, like a play-by-play, but maybe a day or a few days later. Here is an excerpt from this diary.

"So many people have stopped by to see you. People from the sheriff's office, Counts and people from the bank stopped by. One of the girls from the bank brought you some flowers with a card. They would not let her bring the flowers into the ICU, so our daughter took them home and cared for them for you. Even more people have been praying for you. There are people at every corner of the U.S. praying for you and everywhere in

between. I'm quite certain there are even people outside the U.S. who have been praying for you. We have been praying specifically for a whole and complete recovery.

So far, I have been told your heart ejection fraction is only working at 10%, you have some sort of pneumonia and bronchitis. The pneumonia was not visible on any of the x-rays, CT scans or sonograms. The doctors told me these things lead to you going into respiratory arrest which put you into cardiac arrest, this is what caused you to die in the back of the ambulance.

I have been told you will get a heart Cath prior to leaving the hospital so they can see what is causing you to only have 10% ejection fraction. This never happened, they did not do a heart Cath or anything else for your heart. The cardiologists have all told me with an EF of 10% your heart will never heal itself and you will need some sort of mechanical assistance, for your heart, for the rest of your life. Presumably the doctors will do some more tests as time goes by. I do not know for sure what their plans are, I'm not sure they know what the plans are.

So many people are coming by to visit you. Some days it's like a train of people just waiting outside the room to come in. Some days the room is so filled with people I'm afraid the nurses will tell me that I must make people leave, they have not so far. The nurses keep telling me I'm in charge of the room and they will do what I want as far as visitors.

Sarah at this point you are still not conscious; your heart rate and your blood pressure are so bad. One minute they're high the next they are so low it causes great concern. The other night the night shift nurse had to give you a shot because your heart stopped for about 20 seconds. Sarah, I really wish this was all a bad dream and I can wake up shortly beside you in our bed. I wish the doctors could tell me what's going on, but they don't seem to know any more than I do.

God keeps telling me to pray for his will. I cannot, this would mean I would have to give up control and put complete faith in His will being the best. I know this would be best, but I just can't bring myself to do it. Some days I feel like I'm wrestling against all the powers in the world at once. The doctors only give me a little bit of information, I guess that's all they have. I wish I could talk to you about this. You are the one I always go to when things are tough, and now this being the toughest thing I've ever faced and it's all about you. I can't talk to you about it, because you are still in a coma. Sarah, please wake up. Please tell me what's going on. Please tell me what to do. Please tell me everything is going to be okay, in that way you do.

Several days have gone by now, you have been running fevers. I think they have your blood pressure and heart rate under control now. They have changed your medicine several times. It seems like they are just grasping at straws to figure out what is going to work for you. Your blood pressure has reached 220/170 your heart rate has been in the 120's and 130's, but now it's back to a more manageable area.

God still keeps telling me to ask for his will to be done. The other night I pulled my chair/bed right next to your bed and slept next to you holding your arm all night. I did wake up several times though. I kept seeing the shadows of people walking around your bed, this is not uncommon as nurses are in and out all the time. But this time whenever I would wake up to see who was there, there was no one around. I thought my mind was getting the best of me. Until last night, when I saw several Angels surrounding your bed. These Angels were dressed for battle, they had swords and shields. It appeared they were protecting you from something. Oddly enough this comforted me, I was not afraid of them. I'm telling you they were there and were just as clear as though they were human men. Since then, I have seen several Angels around you, this is very comforting.

Your temperature has spiked today. You were running a fever of close to 105 degrees. We had to put ice packs around your neck, under your arms, under your back, under your legs and between your legs. I set a fan to oscillate across your body to help cool you. They gave you so much Tylenol trying to get it to break. It finally broke and you seemed like you might be coming around, but you did not. I'm still hearing God tell me to pray for his will to be done. Sarah, this is getting harder and harder.

I finally broke down on day 10 and prayed for God's will. Well sort of. I asked God if he was going to take you home to do it now, but if he was going to leave with me to bring you back to 100%. This was the single hardest thing I have ever done in my life. I love you so much Sarah. When I got up the next day you began coming out of your coma. You began focusing on things and you began moving your arms and legs around. During the next few days, you had a very rough time. You would thrash around in the bed, I had to put restraints on your hands. The doctor was fearful that you might pull the tube out of your throat. I kept them loose on you because I know how much you hate having your hands restrained.

Over the next several days you did not make much improvement. You kept going in and out of consciousness. I really had no idea what was going to happen. I did hear the voice of God, as audible as I can hear anyone else, tell me that you were going to be okay. I only shared this with pastor.

Sarah, it feels like we have been in the ICU for 3 or 4 forever's. They have run so many tests on you. MRI's, CT's, EEG's and I'm sure I'm missing something. All the tests they run come back with no new information. It seems like every test they run things become more and more confusing. The EEG's showed slow brain activity, but the activity is there. The hospitalist said this is expected, because you have an anoxic brain injury. This is a result of not getting oxygen to your brain for the 6 minutes.

The lung doctor says he's going to extubate you soon (this is when they pull the intubation tube out). He says they will have to put a trach tube in your throat, and then a feeding tube in your stomach. I'm not sure how long you will need these. I am told you may need them for the rest of your life. I don't believe this at all. My belief is we will go home, and you will not have any tubes in you at all."

This is when I stopped keeping a diary. It is so emotional for me to read and to go over. Even today I get teary-eyed and have to take time to gather myself. Please understand this is not about us. It is a story about God's greatness and how He can guide us to be more Christ-like as husbands.

The next hurdle was extubating, removing the intubation tube, from Sarah. They were going to have to do a tracheotomy by placing a "trach tube" in Sarah's neck. They said they needed to do this on or as near day fourteen as possible. The pulmonologist told me if they did not get the intubation tube out around that fourteen-day time frame, there could be irreparable damage to the inside of Sarah's throat. They were actually able to do this on day fifteen but had to wait until her vitals were under control before going to surgery. Then they would put in a feeding tube or "G tube" the following day.

All the medical staff were so confident Sarah would have the trach tube and g tube in for the rest of her life, but I believed the complete opposite. They were so convinced the nurses began teaching me everything I would need to know about feeding Sarah through the g tube and how to take care of it. Likewise, the respiratory therapists taught me more than I would ever want to know about taking care of the trach tube, how to maintain it, and how to clear it. I would become so efficient the nurses would have me take care of her trach tube.

During our time in the ICU, the doctors continually ordered tests and blood drawn for testing. Each test they would run seemed to bring up more questions and provide fewer answers. I was told time and time again her heart was not working right and never would. I was told her brain was not functioning correctly and never would. Sometime during all of this, the hospitalist would determine that Sarah was blind and could not see at all (remember her seeing the angels?). I was told Sarah would be bedridden, that she would never walk, that she would never carry on a normal conversation, that she would have the tubes in for the rest of her life, and that she would basically be a vegetable. Mind you, I have already heard from whom I believe was the greatest physician of all, God, who told me Sarah was going to be okay. So here we go again with my meandering faith.

Some days I would much rather have just found a hole to crawl into and come out only as necessary and wanted absolutely no visitors. On other days I really wanted to have family and friends around. I knew this would ultimately be beneficial for Sarah. I would try to gather myself and keep my eyes on our Jesus, and this seemed much harder some days than others. I would constantly remind myself that God is in control, that God's ways are perfect, and that God's will for us is always better than what we have intended.

A verse I'm sure we all know is **Romans 8:28 And we know that for those who love God all things work together for good, for those who are called according to his purpose.** This does not say everything will work out for good as we want it or see it. In my mind, it can only mean one thing. If God is the only good then it must mean that "...all things work together..." for good as God wants it, for his glory, for his purpose, not ours. This was a tough place to get to and continues to be a hard place to stay in as we continue to struggle with this trial. The next phase would become even harder.

The doctors, led by one meaningful doctor, would make it a daily point to tell me how hopeless Sarah's condition was, even after coming out of her coma. They would no longer suggest that I needed to remove Sarah from all supportive measures, but now they were telling me pointedly that I was simply being mean and cruel by keeping her alive, and the best possible outcome was for me to allow Sarah to pass away peacefully. This continued for many days and hit me like a ton of bricks square in the face. I heard the voice of God tell me Sarah was going to be okay, but I heard the voice of the doctors telling me she was not going to be okay. Did I imagine what I heard from God? Was any of this real? Was there truly any hope? Was this just a nightmare, and would I wake up any second? What is really going on here?

Now my faith had been shaken to the core. I really did not know where I found the strength to get up every morning, where I even found the strength to eat. I needed to have God tell me time and time again that Sarah was going to be okay, but this did not happen. I was in such a dark place I would go to the hospital chapel, a place that seemed always to be empty. I do not know if God allowed me to go when no other people were going or what, but it was nice to have this place to myself. I would repeatedly call Sarah's phone. Oh, it was off, but I wanted to hear her voice. I began to forget what her voice sounded like. This was crazy because she was right there. I could see her, but I forgot what her voice sounded like. I would call and call over and over, just listening to her voice. I was hoping to find some sort of answer in her voice. She has always been so calming to me, and I simply love listening to her. I had to get her advice, but I could not. She was always my rock; she was always where I turned when things got really bad. When all the world was against us, she made everything okay. Now in the worst of times I could not get her opinion. I could not get her advice. What was I supposed to do? What was the right thing? I knew I needed to stop the onslaught of doctors telling me to "pull the plug." I knew what God told me, but where to find this strength?

The absolute last thing I needed was some "holier than thou" coming up and telling me in their pompous tone that, "God would not give you more than you could handle." I knew the opposite to be true, that without God, I could not handle any of this. Even so, I could not find any solace, and I could find no peace. I tried, I prayed and prayed. It seemed my prayers were only going as high as the ceiling. Where was I supposed to turn? I knew where I was supposed to look but could not find the answers.

I'd like to tell you that one day I had an eye-opening experience, and there was some magical scripture that leaped off the pages and smacked me in the face. But none of that happened. It simply took time. It took me studying the Word of God, and I had to ground myself in God's promises. Over time I would come to understand that God did have all of this in His hands, that God had not left me, and He was still right there beside me, mostly carrying me through this horrific time.

One of the things I remember was hearing "Code Blue" called in the ICU. I would later learn this was a code for someone in an immediate life-threatening crisis. Every time I heard "Code Blue" come across the intercom, my heart stopped. I held my breath and waited to hear the room number. I hate to say I was always so happy it was never Sarah's room because that meant some other family was about to have a terrible day. I would always feel kind of guilty for having these thoughts. I knew what kind of struggle I was having as a Christian. I could not figure out how people who did not have God in their lives were actually making it through each day. I guess this is still a lingering question in my mind.

People would comment, "your faith sure is strong. Where do you get such strong faith? You sure must be close to God." In reality, none of that seemed true to me. I felt like I was further away from God than I had ever been. Even today, people comment on how much of an inspiration I am to them. I do not mean to take anything away from any work God is doing, and if He uses me for that work, which is simply why He put on earth, but I really do not see what they see. I see the wretched person and sin-filled heart that I have always been and had. I try to learn more about God and His desire for us. As Martin Luther said, *"We are all mere beggars showing other beggars where to find bread."* This is my hope and prayer that I could show others who God is and what a comfort He is to have in our lives. The Holy Spirit is real, and He really does comfort us. I want to show others where they can find this comfort, and that, as 1 John says, we love Him because He first loved us.

    Eventually, the doctors stopped telling me to "pull the plug." I guess they were satisfied with the DNR I signed. However, my predicament did not change. I still had a wife in the hospital, who was not expected to make it and was given no hope by all the doctors except for one. There was one doctor who would tell me that he was hopeful and was not going to give up. Finally, there was an advocate! I finally had someone I could see and touch who was on my side! He would tell me that if Sarah could be sixty to seventy percent of her previous self, then we could call this successful. Wait, what??? This was not how I prayed. This was not what I asked God for. I asked God for one hundred percent. Here I go again with my back and forth, on again, off again faith. It would take me some time to get to a place where I was fully confident God was going to heal my Sarah. It would be a long road, but one on which I would finally come to realize I was not on alone. I really do not want to take away from the love and support I received from family, friends, and pastors (especially my pastor), but the fact of the matter is I knew only God could heal my wife, and I really needed Him to be as close to me as I heard he had been to others. It took time for me to realize I needed to be the one to move back to God because the reality was God hadn't moved. I did.

Chapter 6
To God Be the Glory

I found ways to pass the time. Obviously, I would read the Bible, and I read the Bible to Sarah. I prayed constantly. I prayed for Sarah's healing, prayed for my strength, and I prayed for God's complete intervention. If you came into Sarah's room for a visit, you were going to pray with me.

I remember one of the sweetest ladies in the whole hospital was one of the housekeepers. She would come into Sarah's room. She wouldn't say much, but she would hum. Sometimes I recognized she was humming an old hymn, and this would bring such a smile to my face. But she still would not say much. I would tell her good morning, or good evening, whichever was applicable. She would respond in like manner. One Sunday when I mustered myself to leave and go to church, I came back not feeling much better than when I left. This sweet lady stopped me and asked for a minute of my time. I was glad to speak with her. She said, "Sir, I don't talk very often while in your wife's room. I can't. Mostly, I can only pray and leave as quickly as possible." I listened very intently as she continued. "I feel the presence of God so thick in her room that I literally cannot say much. I have to leave quickly, so I do not break down and cry in front of y'all." This gave me such comfort and was such a blessing, and I went to Sarah's room and cried. It seemed funny at the time that God would use a lady I didn't even know to boost my faith, to comfort me. Now it seems perfectly normal for complete strangers to comfort us. Angels? I don't know about that, but I know that God will use those willing to be used by Him for His purpose, which sometimes is to comfort others.

Another way I passed the time was just being a husband. I would talk to Sarah, even when she was in her coma, even when she couldn't respond, even when she was not able to hear me or speak back to me. I would talk about current events, family, and just ramble. I had to talk for two.

I would talk to every doctor who came in to check on Sarah. I was full of questions. I'm sure I was on their crazy person list, but I needed answers. Eventually, one of the doctors would tell me that Sarah was ready for physical therapy. I was very confused because she could not even get out of bed. This was the exact reason for the therapy. I was given a list of exercises to do with Sarah while she was in bed. We did these twice every day until we were both exhausted.

Sometimes I felt like I was starring in the movie "Groundhog Day, " where every day was the same day. This was my reality most of the time. I would have to find ways to break this up. I would read to Sarah at different times, and we did her therapy at different times. There were sometimes when they needed to take her for tests or screenings. I really felt alone during these times. I was the only one in her room and could not draw comfort from seeing her. I could not imagine what was going through her mind. She could not talk to me; she could not see me; and she could not communicate at all. She did not know what time it was, and she had no idea, I'm sure, of where she was. This would break my heart every time I thought about it.

Time just kept moving along. Eventually, one day I was told we were going to move out of ICU and go to the fifth floor. I don't know why, but this scared me to death. I knew what we had in the ICU, but I had no idea what to expect when we got to "the floor," as the staff would call it. I asked the doctor if this meant Sarah was out of the woods. He would say she was not critical but in guarded condition.

We moved swiftly, as Sarah was still hooked up to all of her equipment. The staff got Sarah settled rather quickly into her new room. It wouldn't take me long to become comfortable with the staff on the fifth floor. I learned to trust them, and they learned how to deal with me. Once on "the floor," things seemed to move a little quicker. They would bring physical, occupational, and vocational therapists into her room. They would work with her and get her moving. I'm not sure what the actual statistics are, but I was told for every day Sarah was in the bed it would take nine days of recovery to get her moving again. It seemed like an impossible task, but they were up for it and did not hesitate to let me help and become involved.

You see, I was involved in every aspect of Sarah's hospitalization; I assisted whenever and wherever I could. The nurses would eventually tell me that I was one in a thousand. I was not sure what this meant until one day when I asked what they meant. One nurse would tell me that only one in every thousand family members took the level of involvement in their loved one's care that I was taking. This broke my heart to think that nine hundred and ninety-nine patients did not have family members involved in their care. I thought I was doing what everyone did. I would remember our marriage vows and remember the promise I made to Sarah "...in sickness and in health, for better or worse..." I really meant this, and I wanted to do this for my wife. I did not want to sit on the sidelines and let complete strangers care for my wife more than I did. This was unimaginable to me.

One day I was approached by some, what we will call well-meaning social workers from the hospital. They asked me if I had considered a convalescence home for Sarah. I was shocked, and I was very taken aback by this. The old flesh came out in me at this very minute. I looked them directly in the eye and told them Sarah had a home, and it was with me at our home. They continued to insist that I consider the next place Sarah was to go because she would need long-term care. I told them to get out of Sarah's room and never have another conversation with me about this issue. I do not imagine I was very friendly at this point. I was shocked.

I spoke with her primary doctor at the hospital about this. He confirmed that Sarah's stay at the hospital would come to an end sooner rather than later, and I really needed to consider the next move. After my conversation with the social workers, he would not suggest a convalescence home for Sarah but rather an in-patient rehabilitation center. After some consideration, researching, and praying, I decided that one of the local rehab centers would be best for Sarah. I was promptly told this was not an option, as they could not adequately care for her and do the rehabilitation. Again, after much prayer, I stood firm. It was this place or our house, and I would figure things out from there.

One of the representatives from the rehabilitation center was sent to my room, but my suspicion was to tell me that they would not accept Sarah. This wonderful lady came in, spoke with us, got my phone number, and the next day, I got a call from the chief financial officer making arrangements for Sarah to come to their facility.

Now hold on tight. We had been in the hospital where Sarah was not expected ever to leave alive. Then she was not expected to walk, talk, breathe on her own, eat on her own, have a cognitive thought, speak, or move on her own. Then, she was supposed only to be able to go to a convalescence home, and we would not be able to get into the rehabilitation center of my choice. She was leaving the hospital alive, and after having some therapy, moving on her own, and starting to communicate with me. We were now going to the very center that we were not supposed to be able to go to. THANK YOU, JESUS!!!

On Thursday, November 14, 2019, at 4:00 pm, Sarah was taken by ambulance to the rehabilitation center. We got settled in and acquainted with the staff. We were told that the following day, Friday, would be an assessment day, and we would not do much, if anything at all, during the weekend. Therefore, Sarah's therapy would start the following Monday. Also, part of the arrangements was that Sarah would only get one week in the rehabilitation center because we were uninsured and waiting on Medicaid and/or Medicare benefits.

The following morning, we would go to the rehabilitation gym, where the staff would conduct their assessments. They asked me where I thought I would like to see Sarah's progress upon leaving the facility. I, not wanting to ask for the world, would tell them that she would need to be one person assisted in and out of her wheelchair, in and out of the bed and her chair. They asked a bunch of other questions relating to the layout of our home, such as any stairs and so on.

After completing their assessment, the staff returned to me and again asked where I thought I would like to see Sarah's progress upon leaving the facility. We had the same conversation. This was when they began explaining the impossibilities of my expectations. I stood firm with them, and the decision was made to see where we were after her therapy sessions on Monday.

We would do a round robin of speech, occupational, and physical therapy, at least once a day, sometimes twice a day. After the first day, the therapists were impressed with Sarah's drive and determination. After just a few days of therapy, Sarah was actually walking using the parallel bars and some assistance. She was previously given a

Passy Muir valve (the device to put over the trach tube so she could talk). She never got used to using it, so while speech therapy was not going as quickly as physical therapy, occupational therapy did.

The days quickly turned into one week, and just before the end of the week, Sarah was invited to stay for another week. We quickly accepted the invitation and looked forward to the gains she would make. During this week, the staff doctor decided it was time to take Sarah's trach tube out, you know, the thing she was supposed to live with forever. We were very excited to agree but also very anxious and nervous about it. We had been told she would need this to be able to breathe, and now here is a doctor telling us she did not need it any longer. Well, color me surprised.

The next day the trach tube came out. I know you'll find this hard to believe, but there were absolutely no complications. As a matter of fact, she healed rather quickly. We had to start a new therapy; one I have never heard of before: swallow class. They had to teach Sarah how to swallow food and liquid. I have never given this any thought until then. They started with thickened liquid, the same consistency she received while having the trach tube. This would quickly turn to Sarah being able to drink coffee, one of her loves, and eating breakfast with me, one of my loves.

Next thing we knew, the end of the week is upon us, and Sarah is again offered another week of therapy. We again humbly accepted. This was the week of Thanksgiving, and we were to spend Thanksgiving away from home. Even though the kids would come up and bring food from home, this was hard for both of us. We tried to make the best of it, and the facility actually had a great Thanksgiving meal. Sarah was then offered a fourth week at the facility. This was amazing to us how one week turned into four.

By the end of Sarah's therapy, she was walking, using a walker, from her room to therapy and back. This was made more difficult by the fact she was still blind and could not see the route to take. I learned quickly how to guide her so she could continue to make these strides. She was also walking up and down the therapy stairs and had begun talking directly from the speech therapy. We were so excited for the progress, but even more than that, we had several opportunities to witness to the staff. We left the facility, in our car, on December 12, 2019, and were home for Christmas. What a Christmas this would be! It would not be one of many gifts or grandeur, but I had my Sarah, and the kids had their mama home for Christmas. Just a few months prior, this was an impossible prospect, one I was told would never happen.

Before leaving the rehabilitation center, I had to remodel our bedroom and bathroom. I had to have it fully handicap acceptable. This was not a cheap endeavor, but God had everything covered. I then was also facing many, many dollars' worth of medical bills. There was almost seven hundred and fifty thousand dollars' worth of medical bills. I figured it was a cheap price to pay for my wife, and again was trusting God to take care of it. Within just a few months, the hospital let us know that their entire bill of over five hundred thousand dollars had been taken care of. I still do not know who God used to take care of this. I figure that's between them.

So, to take stock of where we are, Sarah was not supposed to live, but she's alive. She was then not supposed to walk, talk, breathe or eat on her own. She does all of these, and we have never had one piece of medical equipment in our house to assist her with anything other than walking. She was not supposed to ever get out of bed, have a conversation or a cognitive thought. Her heart was in horrible shape and would need mechanical assistance for Sarah to survive. These are all healed. We are grateful for the doctors and their knowledge, and we do not take anything away from them and their abilities. We understand that God is within His right to use whom He chooses when He chooses to accomplish His desire and His will.

Oh, I forgot to mention the small fact that after getting home and the New Year passed, Sarah had an appointment with her cardiologist. They ran another echocardiogram to determine the most plausible type of mechanical assistance for Sarah. After the test, the doctor's office called and said they were not sure what was going on, but her ejection fraction was at fifty percent. As a reference, a normal EF is forty-five to seventy percent. Remember, her heart, with an EF of ten percent, was not supposed to be able to heal. Praise God, and Praise God.

God had defied all the common medical knowledge of the day and healed Sarah. God, and God alone is responsible for this healing. The doctors, who gave no hope, cannot take the glory, but only God can have the glory and the honor, which is where it should all go anyway.

Chapter 7
He's Still Working on Me

In the months and years since Sarah's "heart attack," (this is how we refer to her medical crisis) things have still been a roller coaster ride. We have been to a Neuro Ophthalmologist, which I had never heard of before. This is a very specific specialty, the one we visited was about an hour and a half away from our house, the closest to us.

They were so kind and awesome. They ran all kinds of tests and took pictures of Sarah's eyes I had no idea was possible. At the end of the day, he found nerve damage to both of Sarah's eyes. He would tell us her brain was not the issue, but the nerve damage would not be able to heal. He said the fact that she was without oxygen for the 6 minutes caused the nerve damage. Sarah's faith seems to continue to dwarf mine. She looked the doctor in the eye, told him "Thank you and said I look forward to 'seeing' you someday". Even still, this was absolutely the longest ride home. We ran the gamut of emotions the entire way. We would say this seems to line up with what the other doctors said about Sarah not being able to make it. We said we still believed God was going to restore her sight this side of heaven. We cried and got upset, prayed, talked to friends and family, and felt defeated but, mostly, we wanted God to take the darkness from her eyes.

Sarah has also been seeing a neurologist, who has been wonderful. He tells us that her brain will likely heal completely of the anoxia, but it will take a long time. He said the anoxia is similar to a stroke patient, but the main difference is with a stroke patient, the damage is usually irreparable as the stroke part of the brain is normally dead.

However, with anoxia, the brain is not damaged beyond repair, but due to the complex nature of the brain, it takes a very long time to heal and may take several years.

We notice, on a regular basis, improvements in Sarah's brain. Her speech, one of the main things affected by the anoxia, has improved greatly. Her thought process has never been better, and her dexterity is still improving.

I had a bit of savings and was making more money than I had ever made before. When this happened, I did not work for several months. This, along with the bills, continued appointments, and medication Sarah required (all without insurance), took it all. I went to zero in the bank and in my retirement account. I do not tell you this looking for any sort of sympathy. God has not let us lose anything or go hungry.

I did have to make several adjustments. After being retired for several years, I had to go back to work at the sheriff's office, where I could have the guarantee of a steady paycheck and insurance for Sarah. Even though she did qualify for social security disability, the Medicare portion would not kick in for twenty-four months after the initial qualifications, not from the date of injury. We all know how quickly the government is to work with us. This took nine or eight forever's. Going back to work like this was never even a passing thought for me. I really was enjoying the freedoms that come with being retired. I was also enjoying not having to work near as much as I had in the past. Now, I am back to work in a job I never wanted to be back in, for reasons I would never have imagined possible, but through it all, God is faithful. We just need to take a minute to realize just how faithful He is by the things He has kept from us.

Sarah went from being the most independent person I have ever known to being the most dependent person I have ever known. I do many things now that were never in my wheelhouse before. We shared the household chores before, and by that, I mean she did them, and I did what I thought were chores outside the house. I have learned that I rather enjoy being able to go outside and take care of those things. I had to make a lot of changes personally and professionally. There are so many sacrifices I have had to make because of all of this. Please do not think I am griping or complaining. I am actually very honored to be able to take care of my Sarah. I am very blessed that she is here for me to be able to take care of. Even though there are things that I now do that I never thought of doing before, I can tell you without any hesitation that God is good.

    I would like to tell you that as of writing this, everything is back to the way it was before. First of all, it will never be like before, but, secondly, we now have a new normal in our lives. Sarah has to sacrifice the things she used to do—her independence and her vision. So, I feel fairly comfortable telling you I have the easy part of all this.

    I have learned how to live with a blind spouse, but Sarah has learned how to live blind. I have had to pick up extra chores, but Sarah cannot do the "simple" things anymore. I have had to go back to work, but Sarah cannot leave the house without someone else.

I have had to become more familiar with feminine things (like hairspray, mousse, hair scrunchies, earrings, and the sort), but Sarah has had to learn how to take care of herself all over again, this time without the benefit of her vision.

The "sacrifices" I have to make are actually just fulfilling the promise I made to her on February 11, 1994, when I told her that I would love her and cherish her through richer and poorer, through sickness and health in good times and bad until death do us part. By God's grace, I did not have to deal with the "until death do us part." I do count it as a blessing and a joy to be able to take care of her. I look at all that has happened and can tell you James 1:2-4

> ***Count it all joy, my brothers, when you meet trials of various kinds, for you know that the testing of your faith produces steadfastness. And let steadfastness have its full effect, that you may be perfect and complete, lacking in nothing.***

is possible to live by. This is a hard place to get to and an even harder place to stay, but Philippians 4:13 reminds us of our strength in Christ. We also have the assurance that our suffering will not last forever.

> ***And after you have suffered a little while, the God of all grace, who has called you to his eternal glory in Christ, will himself restore, confirm, strengthen, and establish you. 1 Peter 5:10***

While I do not know how long a little while is, I do have confidence in God's promise.

Sarah continues to improve, but more importantly, she continues to challenge me to be a better Christian, husband, father, and grandpa. When I get down, and it does happen quite often, she will ask me very bluntly, "Has God not proved Himself enough?" Talk about humbling. When your wife, who has literally gone through hell on earth, can, with a straight face, rebuke you for your lack of faith, it shows how much further we have to go.

I pray every day, even as we continue our struggle, for God to intervene on our behalf and bring comfort to us. We have every belief that while we are still on this earth, God is going to restore Sarah's vision. We just keep holding onto the faith and put our hope in Jesus and the blood He shed for us on the cross. God has never made one promise that the walk of a Christian would be easy or that it would be without its perils. On the contrary, He has made it plainly clear that it would not be easy. Jesus told His disciples in John 15:18-19

If the world hates you, know that it has hated me before it hated you. If you were of the world, the world would love you as its own; but because you are not of the world, but I chose you out of the world, therefore the world hates you.

As I told you early on, my goal for writing this was not to boast about what we have done, how great our faith is, or how great we are. My intended purpose for writing this was to show how great God is, how faithful He is, and how He can help you get through even the toughest times in our lives. God promises that He will never leave us or forsake us. He promises to love us, and He proves this time and time again.

So how does all of this apply to being a Godly husband and having faith? The short answer is I don't know. What I do know is that God has entrusted me with Sarah, and per His instructions, I am commanded to love her like Christ loved the church, which is His bride. We know Christ gave His life for the church so He could have a perfect bride. This is told to us in scripture.

So that he might present the church to himself in splendor, without spot or wrinkle or any such thing, that she might be holy and without blemish.
Ephesians 5:27

I do not want anyone to get the wrong ideas. I am not claiming to be some great man of God or the founder of some great faith-based programs, nor am I a great theologian or an elder with years and years of experience as a marriage counselor or a pastor (I am not a pastor). As a matter of fact, I am the proud recipient of a general education high school diploma, with only some college courses under my belt, who struggles daily to live the Christian life. I need you to understand that I am constantly striving for more knowledge of God, to get my relationship with Him right so that my relationships on earth can be right. I am aiming for God to make me a better husband, a better dad, and a better grandpa. I have to work on this daily.

    I did not receive any grand revelations during this. I was not given any supernatural strength other than what we all receive through the shed blood of Jesus Christ. I have only discovered what has been around for millennia, that Christ is real and that He really can help us if we only let Him. I have learned to be more dependent on God for everything. I have learned to be grateful for each and every day I have with Sarah. I have learned to cherish every moment. I have learned that I am definitely imperfect and need God's help in every aspect of my life.

I have been told the way I love and have loved Sarah through this, and the strength I have demonstrated is an inspiration to others. I don't know anything about all of that. What I do know is I never thought I would have to love Sarah through this type of "sickness" and "worst of times." I loved her enough in 1994 to promise her I would love her through these times should they come, and I know I love her more today than I did then. I know God gives me strength each day to make it through another day, as I see her with her struggles. I still have a hard time watching the most independent person I have ever known have difficulty doing daily tasks. I know her spirit, her love for God, and her positive, Godly attitude are an inspiration to me.

I thank God every day for Sarah, for the opportunity to love her, and the privilege of taking care of her in her times of need. I will say she has done a fabulous job of learning how to live her life all over again. I did not realize how much more struggle it would be for me to adjust to our new life than it was for

Sarah. My heart continues to break when I see her struggle with small things, with things she used to do without any thought.

I still look forward to seeing her every time I come home. My heart still has a pitter-patter to it whenever I see her. I'm sure I aggravate her most of the time, as I have become a "helicopter" husband. I want to protect her from any further harm or prevent her from having difficulties. I have not been doing a stellar job at letting her achieve things on her own, and this is an area where I have to learn to let go. I want to love her and be the best husband I can be for her.

I do not love and care for Sarah because I have to, because of some sort of guilty conscience, a ceremony, or some social obligation. It is a privilege to love her and take care of her. I love her because she won my heart. I love her because she tolerates my annoying traits and does not complain much. I love her because of her gentle spirit and loving heart, and I love her because of her attitude and the way she treats people with love. I love her because she is everything I am not, and I love her because she loves me back, without any conditions or expectations.

I would be negligent if I didn't mention the fact that God has richly blessed us in many ways during our hardship, but one of the most precious blessings has been the wonderful gift of a beautiful granddaughter. Almost one year to the day of Sarah's heart attack God blessed our family with this awesome little girl. When I see her and Sarah interact, I know only God is able, He alone holds the keys to our Joy and Happiness. He alone has the ability to turn our thinking around and show us what is really important in this life.

I hope I have been able to show you God and how we can accomplish anything with God's help, and by surrendering to God's will and seeking Him, we can become Godly husbands even when our faith sometimes turns to doubt.

As a final word of encouragement when you are in the valley. Remember we are never there alone as we are reminded in Psalm 23:4-6

Yeah, though I walk through the valley of the shadow of death I will fear no evil for you are with me your rod and your staff they comfort me. You prepare a table before me in the presence of my enemies, you anoint my head with oil, my cup overflows, surely goodness and mercy shall follow me all the days of my life and I will dwell in the house of the Lord forever.

This has been Sarah's scripture during these times. She routinely quotes this passage, especially when she is at a low. Thank God that does not happen very often anymore.

I leave you with the comforting words of Paul in II Thessalonians 3:16&18:

Now may the Lord of peace himself give you peace at all times in every way. The Lord be with you all. The grace of our Lord Jesus Christ be with you all.

Made in the USA
Middletown, DE
03 September 2024